Kirklees
METROPOLITAN · COUNCIL

Culture + Leisure Services
Red Doles Lane
Huddersfield, West Yorks. HD2 1YF

D BE RETURNED OI ORE THE LATEST
N.
THE ITEM IS

ONE

D0835786

the **Cockatiel**

Feeding, care, buying, accommodation,

breeding, health and lots more about

the Cockatiel

Contents

Foreword   4

General   6
   A little history   6
   What species of bird is the Cockatiel?   6
   Where does the Cockatiel come from and how
   does it live there?   7
   Is there a visible difference between
   a male and a female?   8
   What colour are young Cockatiels? 11

Buying 12
   Things to consider first 12
   One Cockatiel or two? 13
   Things to look out for 15

Accommodation 16
   Cage dimensions 16
   The most suitable place 16
   How should I furnish it? 17
   How often should it be cleaned? 19

Behaviour and handling 22
   The Cockatiel's character 22
   The Cockatiel's body language 22
   What is moulting? 22
   Getting used to the surroundings 23
   Does a Cockatiel need a name? 24
   How do I tame my Cockatiel? 24
   How do I teach it to speak? 26
   Can I let a Cockatiel fly around the room? 26

Feeding 30
   What do they need? 30
   Which food can I best give in practice? 37
   What is pellet food? 38

Cockatiels in other colours 42
    Pastel 42
    White-faced 42
    Pied 42
    Black-eyed white and/or yellow 42
    Albino 43
    Lutino 43
    Cinnamon 43
    Pearl 43

Health and sickness 44
    Recognising a sick bird 44
    Why do sick birds fluff their feathers? 45
    Sicknesses and disorders 45
        Anaemia 45
        Blood mite (red bird mite) 46
        Intestinal infection (enteritis) 46
        Diarrhoea 48
        Overgrown beak 48
        Catching a cold 50
        Crop disease 50
        Egg-binding 51
        Eye infections 51
        Ornithosis 52
        Leg fractures 52
        Psittacosis 53
        Knemidokoptic mange 53
        Feather lice and feather mites 53
        Injuries 55
        Wing fractures 55
        Worms 56
    Bird euthanasia 56
    Disinfectants and pesticides 56
    What are the requirements of a hospital cage? 57
    Making your own hospital cage 58

Profile 64

Foreword

The Cockatiel is one of the most popular and best
loved cage and aviary birds amongst bird fanciers.
This beautiful bird with its characteristic crest has a
placid, even-tempered character.
The fact that its care is undemanding, that it adapts
well to captivity and quickly bonds with its keeper, has
contributed to its popularity. It is therefore hardly
surprising that many bird fanciers each year decide to
buy one of these beautiful birds.

This book is an excellent guide for Cockatiel
beginners. The most important aspects of the hobby
addressed are such things as what you need to look out
for when you are buying, which is the most suitable
accommodation and the care and handling
requirements. Naturally, a chapter is dedicated to
health and sicknesses. In short it is a valuable work of
reference for every Cockatiel fancier.

We wish you much pleasure, not only while reading
this book but also with your bird(s). It is and it remains
a wonderful hobby!

About Pets

A Publication of About Pets.

ISBN 1852792035
First printing
September 2003
Second printing
December 2004

Original title: *de Valkparkiet*
Adri van Kooten
© 2003 Welzo Media Productions bv,
About Pets bv
Warffum, the Netherlands
http://www.aboutpets.info

Photos:
Rob Dekker,
Adri van Kooten,
Piet Onderdelinden
and Jan de Nijs

Printed in China through Printworks Int. Ltd.

General

John Gould first described the Cockatiel in his book 'The Birds of Australia'. This well-known ornithologist visited Australia between 1838 and 1840.

Habitat of the Cockatiels in Australia

He travelled with his wife who added beautiful illustrations to the book.

A little history
Cockatiels must have been very prolific in Australia around 1839 because in his book John Gould wrote that the ground was strewn with Cockatiels and that hundreds sat together on tree branches. Not long after John Gould described the Cockatiel, large numbers started to be imported into Europe. The first breeding successes came in Germany in 1850.

The first Dutch Cockatiel chicks were born in captivity in 1865 and the first in Belgium in 1870. The Cockatiel was given its scientific name *Nymphicus hollandicus* in

1956. 'Nymphicus' meaning: nymph-like and 'hollandicus': from Holland, the old name for Australia. Its scientific name therefore means 'beautifully slim bird from Australia'. Anybody who gets to know this magnificent bird will immediately realise that the Cockatiel is worthy of its scientific name.

What species of bird is the Cockatiel?
Many ornithologists consider the Cockatiel to be a separate species. This is because no other bird is comparable with the Cockatiel's appearance and behaviour. There is, for example, not a single cockatoo, parrot or parakeet with the same unique plumage combination of grey, white and yellow.

Where does the Cockatiel come from and how does it live there?

The Cockatiel originated in Australia where it is found in all but the coastal areas of the North, the East, the South and part of the West, although recent research has shown that the Cockatiel is spreading closer to the coast. The main reason being that primarily the young are leaving their parents to live elsewhere because of a scarcity of food.

Social behaviour

Cockatiels often live in the wild as pairs in groups of ten or twelve birds. Groups of several hundred birds are however not uncommon.

They have no specific habitat which means that they can be found in open wooded savannahs, in trees bordering flowing water, in desert-like grass-covered land and in city parks. They are not normally found in thick forests. Cockatiels lead essentially nomadic lives dictated by the availability of sufficient drinking water and food, which is why they are often found around rivers, creeks and small brooks.

Cockatiels spend much of the day on the ground in groups foraging for food. The birds have developed an alarm system. To be able to keep the surrounding area under observation, a number of birds

occupy strategic lookout posts high up while the majority are feeding. Whenever danger threatens, the lookouts warn the other birds with harsh warning calls so that they can make their escape. When everything appears to be safe again, the group returns to the ground to continue looking for food.

Breeding period

In southern Australia, the Cockatiel mainly breeds in the period from August to December and in the north from April to June. The Cockatiel breeds throughout the year in central Australia depending upon the weather. Birds pair for life.

Nesting places

In their natural habitat, Cockatiels breed in holes in the thick branches and trunks of eucalyptus trees. Each pair's breeding hole is often separated by more than 650 feet (200m) from their nearest neighbour. Pairs will never breed in the same tree as another pair. Their preference is for a breeding place with a wide field of vision. This behaviour also occurs in cap-tivity. Cockatiels don't like deep nest boxes. No, they clearly have a preference for a shallow nest from which they can keep a good lookout! Cockatiels are most often found in open areas where they can keep their surroundings under observation from the branches of eucalyptus trees. Because the bark

Couples stay together for their whole life

of the eucalyptus trees is grey with white flecks, the birds are difficult to spot.

Food

In the wild Cockatiels feed on ripe and unripe seeds from grasses and weeds. They also eat blossom nectar from flowering eucalyptus trees, berries, nuts, leaf buds and a variety of insects and larvae. Their preference for leaf buds is apparent when you provide them with privet branches (with leaves) in the aviary. They are crazy about them. I never forget my Cockatiels when I'm cutting the privet hedge. In the wild, they like to congregate in areas where grain is being cultivated.

Is there a visible difference between a male and a female?

Before answering this question it's important for you to know that amongst bird fanciers the male and female birds are called cock and hen respectively. To return to the question however: yes, there is a clear difference between the Cockatiel cock and the hen. The difference is primarily in the colour.

The cock's colours

The cock's body feathers are chiefly a deep dark grey colour. The forehead, cheeks and neck are yellow. The crest is also yellow running out to a black tip. The cock has a large orange red ear patch on each cheek.

The underside of the tail is black whereas the wings are predominantly a deep dark grey colour. In addition, the cock has broad white wing edges that makes it look as though it has partially white shoulders and wings. The irises of the eyes are black and the beak and legs are grey. The cock is about 13 inches (34 cm) tall.

The hen's colours

Both the colour and markings of the hen's body feathers are generally much lighter than the cock's and her head is a much greyer colour. The hen's crest is predominantly light grey in colour. A clear colour difference can also be seen in the orange/red ear patch: it's clearly less intense in hens. An important difference between cocks and hens is the tail. The underside of the hen's tail displays irregular yellow stripes whilst the cock's is black.

The hen is about the same size as the cock, from experience actually often a little broader.

Other differences

An important difference between the cock and the hen is the cock's macho behaviour and mating song. The "macho" behaviour displays itself primarily by the cock very perkily walking up and down the perch or the floor of the cage or aviary with partially spread wings. The cock often combines the physical behaviour with a mating song, a melodious sounding tune. Hens don't display this behaviour.

What colour are young Cockatiels?

All young Cockatiels look like hens so it's difficult to tell the difference between cocks and hens until they are about six months old when yellow feathers appear on the young cocks' heads and sexing them by colour becomes possible. Having said that, young cocks often start to sing a courtship song at four months of age, so from that moment these at least are distinguishable from the young hens. Young Cockatiels are fully coloured within one year and it is then difficult to distinguish them from their parents. Sexing birds of this age shouldn't present any difficulties.

Buying

Although the Cockatiel is undemanding when it comes to its care, it is nevertheless important that a number of aspects are carefully considered before deciding to buy one or maybe more birds.

Young Cockatiels

Things to consider first

Take the following points into consideration if you are thinking about buying one or more Cockatiels:

- If you are considering buying the birds simply because the children like them, it's important to realise that the interest and enthusiasm of a child can be short-lived. In practice, it is very often the parents that end up looking after the birds.
  You need to decide for yourself if you are prepared to do this should it be necessary.
- Cockatiels can live to a ripe old age. As long as they remain healthy, they can easily live for 15 years or more. You need to take this into careful consideration too.
- Allergy to feathers and dust. It's important to find out if anybody in the household is especially sensitive to dust and feathers. In such cases buying a Cockatiel can result in an increase in health problems for the person affected, requiring you to get rid of the bird.
- Cockatiels make a mess. There will be a regular mess around the cage consisting of peeled seeds, sand, feathers, and dust. If the bird is regularly allowed to fly around the room some droppings might occasionally end up on the carpet or furniture. If you can't live with the idea, you need to ask yourself if a Cockatiel really is the right animal for you.
- Cockatiels make 'noise'. Just like other birds, Cockatiels regularly make themselves heard. Sometimes the noise they

produce is a soft 'chatter' but now and again they like to be more vocal. If peace and quiet is important, you will need to take this behaviour into account.

One Cockatiel or two?

A Cockatiel is a flocking bird and it can't cope well living on its own. If the home is normally deserted during the day, you can best buy two Cockatiels so that the birds at least have each other as constant companions. This will keep them lively and provide them with the necessary stimulation. Whether you choose two cocks or two hens makes no difference but in the event that you choose two birds of the same sex, one will behave like a cock and the other like a hen. The most natural solution remains a cock and hen pair.

Two birds will however become tame slower than a single bird. If you choose to buy only one bird then you need to realise that the bird will need a lot of attention, a minimum of a couple of hours a day, every day. If you don't give it the attention it needs, it will become bored and progressively less active. You will also need to invest a lot of attention and time if you want to make a bird hand-tame.

Things to look out for

Cockatiels can be bought from pet shops and breeders, but breeders will generally be able to offer a wider choice and often at slightly lower prices. Nevertheless, good birds can often be bought at pet shops.

When you are buying your Cockatiel be sure to pay special attention to the following points:

• The most important aspect is the condition of the bird you are intending to buy. A healthy bird is active and its plumage fits snugly about its body. The eyes should be shiny and it should show interest in everything happening around it. A bird that is feeling poorly will often sit quietly in a corner with fluffed feathers and dull eyes.

• Always view the bird(s) to be purchased from a distance, never stand over the cage. The majority of birds find this highly threatening. Even the sickest bird will pull its feathers tightly against its body as a reaction.

• Look to see if the feathers around the anus are clean. If they are fouled with droppings it could indicate diarrhoea, a sign that the bird is not healthy.

• Always buy a bird with a leg ring. A leg ring indicates that a breeder registered with the bird federation has bred the bird. The leg ring should show the breeder's registration number, a serial number and most importantly the bird's year of birth. It is important to buy a young bird because young birds are easier to tame than older birds. By a young bird I mean a bird that is ten weeks old.

• Don't forget to examine the bird's breast with your fingers. The breastbone must not feel sharp. If it does then the bird is too thin and probably sick.

• Observe the bird's behaviour. Is it sitting quietly on its perch? It is better not to buy a bird that is very restless because this characteristic is difficult to counteract and tends to remain with it for the rest of its life.

• Ask the shop salesperson and/or the breeder about the method of feeding and for the product names of the seed, egg food and strength food that the bird is being given. This can be useful background information.

• Never buy a bird just to avoid returning home with empty hands. Buying a bird needs to be done with care. Ask yourself if the bird meets the requirements and your wishes. This will avoid your having to make 'regrettable decisions' in the birdcage or aviary.

Accom-modation

Cockatiels can be accommodated in the living room in a roomy cage or indoor aviary. Bear in mind that a cage must offer the bird(s) enough space.

Cage dimensions

A cage measuring 40 x 24 x 32 inches (100 cm x 60 cm x 80 cm) L x W x H. for example is adequate housing for one or two Cockatiels. A larger cage, for example an indoor aviary, is naturally always better. It is inadvisable to use a cage with dimensions smaller than those mentioned above.

The most suitable place

When choosing a suitable location for a cage or aviary, it is most important to ensure that it will not stand in a draught. A draughty location will inevitably result in sickness and in the worst case the birds' death!
You should never place a birdcage close to open or draughty windows or doors! Place the cage or aviary for example against a solid wall so that one of the sides faces onto a (large) window. Remember, there must be no danger from draughts!

If placed in front of a window the bird will have the diversion of things going on outside as well as inside the house. Another advantage of being placed close to a window is that the bird will experience a natural day/night rhythm. A Cockatiel may never be subjected to intense sunlight or be placed in the direct vicinity of a heater. Cockatiels don't like this at all. Make sure that a shady place is always available in the cage for the bird to make use of. Position the cage or aviary at a height that makes good eye contact possible between the bird and keeper because this will help in building trust.

How should I furnish it?

A Cockatiel's accommodation naturally needs furnishing

Perches

One of the most important items in a cage or aviary is the perches. The majority of the perches must be thick enough to ensure that the bird's toes can only close three quarters of the way around them. To prevent the birds developing corns it's important to fit perches of differing diameters. After all, branches in the wild are not all of the same thickness. You can choose between plastic and hardwood perches but natural ones, like willow branches for example, are good. The advantage with hardwood and plastic perches is that that they are easy to clean. The advantage of natural perches is that they also answer the bird's need to gnaw things and they are easily replaced by new ones. Don't place perches too low. Birds, and therefore Cockatiels as well, like to sit as far above the ground as possible.

Feeding bowls

You can best use metal, plastic or earthenware feeding bowls for your bird(s). These bowls are easy to clean and they can take a lot of punishment from the Cockatiel's strong beak. Make sure that the bowls can be fixed to the bars. Hang them up so that the birds can easily reach them from a perch. Always hang them in pairs; one for seed and the other for greens, egg food, fruit and the like.

Drinking fountains

You can best use a drinking fountain to supply water. This is an inverted bottle with an angled drinking tube projecting from the base. The bottle can be fixed to the outside of the bars by using a mounting bracket with the drinking tube projecting through the bars. Make sure that it is fixed securely in place. The drinking fountain must be refilled daily and disinfected at least once a week. The simplest way to disinfect a drinking fountain is to immerse it in a bleach solution (follow the instructions) for a day or two. This method means of course that you will need to buy two drinking fountains so that you always have one to use while the other is being disinfected.

Feeding bowls

Cage litter

Spreading a layer of suitable material over the bottom of the birdcage or indoor aviary will make it easy to remove droppings. A number of materials can be used such as chicken grit, sand and/or beech chippings. One of the advantages of chicken grit is that it also provides the birds with all sorts of elements, such as minerals. Another advantage is that the floor nearly always looks clean. Chicken grit, as opposed to sand or beech chippings, will stay put once spread. Beech chippings offer the birds the advantage of having something to nibble on to combat boredom.

The most frequently used cage litter is actually shell sand, also known as bird sand, which can be obtained from pet shops. In many cases manufacturers add (bird) grit. The importance of grit for the Cockatiel's body is described in the chapter Feeding. It is best not to use newspapers as cage litter because digestion problems can occur in birds that eat it. Using newspapers can also lead to a lot of mess being created. Some Cockatiels have great fun tearing newspapers into tiny shreds.

Toys
It is important to keep Cockatiels busy. Boredom can lead to all sorts of unpleasant complaints such as feather plucking. Pet shops stock all sorts of suitable toys that are sure to keep a Cockatiel happy. There are bells, mirrors, climbing sticks, perch

swings and much more. A mirror, especially, can provide a lot of amusement. The Cockatiel will recognise the image it sees in the mirror as being one of its own kind and react accordingly. Make sure that toys are made of strong material, such as metal, plastics or hardwood.

A shower or bath?

Some Cockatiels love bathing, and if a bath is made available they will use it regularly. The majority of Cockatiels however

are crazy about a daily shower. You can best shower a Cockatiel with a plant spray filled with warm water. Immediately after the shower the bird will start cleaning itself and when the feathers are completely dry it will look magnificent. A regular shower is very beneficial for a Cockatiel's general condition so it is a good idea to give it one regularly, preferably several times a week.

Is a nesting box necessary?

Cockatiels normally sleep on a perch so they don't necessarily need a nesting box. A nesting box only needs to be hung up in the cage or aviary if there are plans to start breeding. In the case of a cock and hen pair, simply hanging up a nesting box is often enough to stimulate breeding.

How often should it be cleaned?

The feeding bowls and drinking fountain should be cleaned daily. The drinking fountain should be disinfected weekly with bleach according to the instructions on the bottle. The layer of sand, beech chippings and/or chicken grit on the floor of the cage should be replaced weekly.

If the cage contains more than one bird, the cage litter will need to be replaced more often. The perches and toys should also be cleaned and disinfected once a month, for example.

Nesting box

Behaviour and handling

This beautiful bird with its characteristic crest has a placid, even-tempered character.

The Cockatiel's character

Cockatiels by their nature are placid and even-tempered and therefore ideal birds to take into your home. Their placid nature also means that they accept a partner quite quickly. They will virtually never react in an aggressive way towards family or visitors. They are also friendly towards other varieties of birds and are therefore suitable for keeping in mixed aviaries.

Cockatiel's body language

A sick bird often behaves differently to a healthy bird so it's important for you to know what the Cockatiel's normal behaviour is. Normal behaviour is:
• Sharpening the beak. A Cockatiel likes to clean its beak by rubbing it along a perch.

When they do this it looks as if they are sharpening it.
• Sitting on one leg. If a Cockatiel feels relaxed it will sit on one leg. This is a sign that it is feeling well. It also sits on one leg when it sleeps. An adult Cockatiel that sleeps on two legs is sick!
• Feather-shaking. A Cockatiel regularly shakes its feathers to rearrange them. A bird will also shake its feathers after a shock as an indication that it's relaxing.
• Head in the feathers. A Cockatiel sleeps with its head buried in its feathers. This is a Cockatiel's normal sleeping position.

What is moulting?

During the moult the bird replaces old feathers with new

feathers. Many birds complete their moult within six to seven weeks. Birds mostly moult twice a year. The first moulting period takes place in spring and the second somewhere in August and September. Due to the need to produce new feathers, birds have an increased requirement for animal protein. You can assist during moulting by providing them with extra animal protein, such as brown bread soaked in milk, egg food and strength food. Spraying them daily with a plant spray will also assist the moult. If adequate feeding and housing are provided year-round however, the moult will generally be problem-free.

Getting used to the surroundings

Make sure that the cage is fully furnished and standing in the right location before you release your newly bought bird into it. The carton transport box should be carefully positioned in front of the cage opening and the bird should be left to fly out without assistance. If the bird is frightened, you may need to help it by grasping it gently and releasing it into the cage. In most cases, the bird will end up sitting in a sad heap on the floor in a corner of the cage. This is quite normal and you shouldn't be too concerned about it. You can best leave the bird alone for the first few hours. Try to stay away

from the area of the cage completely because the bird will be somewhat nervous and easily frightened.

After a while, the bird's self confidence will return and it will start to explore the surroundings. Don't worry if it doesn't eat or drink anything in the first few hours. This is normal. The bird will only start to eat a little seed from the feeding bowl when it has started to get used to the new surroundings. If things go well it will soon be sitting on a perch shaking out its feathers. By shaking out its feathers, the bird is literally shaking off any nervousness. As soon as you have the impression that the bird is feeling safe in its cage, you can carefully try to make contact. Don't get too close to the cage but talk to the bird in a relaxed voice from about three feet away. Repeat its name as much as possible and don't make any sudden movements. The bird will get used to your company and the presence of other members of the household over time and become progressively less nervous.

In the beginning, you can best approach the bird in the morning. The bird will not have eaten during the night so may well accept something from you like a piece of fruit or greens. If it will not eat from your hand you can push the food between the bars. Try again each morning to see if it will eat out of your hand. Remember that perseverance (eventually) wins.

Does a Cockatiel need a name?

It is a good idea to give the bird(s) a name. If you always use its name, it will quickly learn to associate the sound with itself and it won't be long before it reacts when its name is called. Be sure to choose a short name. If the bird turns out to be a talented speaker, it will soon be able to say its own name.

How do I tame my Cockatiel?

Cockatiels can best be tamed and taught to speak before they are three months old. It is even better to remove young from the nest just before they are ready to fly when they are about four weeks old, although you will still need to feed them with the help of a food syringe at this age. It will not be quite so easy to tame older birds or teach them to speak.

No other birds should be present while you are doing hand-taming or speech training. Hand-taming a Cockatiel as such is not that difficult. If you regularly offer a Cockatiel one of your fingers to use as a perch, hand-taming will not present you with any problems. Try not to grasp a bird with a whole hand because birds find large grasping hands very

threatening. Let the bird fly free around the room. A young Cockatiel is generally very inquisitive and if it's allowed to fly, it will often land on the keeper. Take a few precautions before giving a bird the freedom to fly. Close windows and doors and take into consideration the presence of any hot objects, electric cables and toxic houseplants!

How do I teach it to speak?

Speech training stands the best chance of succeeding when a bird is the member of a family, meaning that the whole family needs to be involved in taming the Cockatiel and teaching it to speak.

Speech is best taught by repeating the same (short) words in the same tone, every day, as many times a day as possible. Speech training, as opposed to taming, can be done by an individual. A woman's voice is preferable. A cassette recorder can be very useful in teaching a Cockatiel to speak because it can be switched on when there is nobody at home. Short words containing a lot of vowels are best such as: Coco, hello etc.

Although in principle both male and female birds have a tendency to imitate sounds they hear, it is preferable to train males because they are less aggressive and in general easier to teach than females. You need to realise though that endless patience is necessary to teach a bird to speak. Birds can go for weeks and sometimes months without uttering a single word only to surprise you when they finally start to speak.

Can I let a Cockatiel fly around in the room?

Giving a Cockatiel the freedom to fly is actually necessary if you want to keep the bird in good condition. Flying ensures that it uses its flight muscles that otherwise remain unused in the cage.

How do I let the Cockatiel fly around in a room?

Before letting the bird fly around the room it needs to have become acclimatised to its cage at home over a period of at least three weeks. By keeping it confined during this time, the Cockatiel will come to accept the cage as its home. Apart from being the place where it can sit quietly and sleep, it is also the place where it knows

it can eat and drink. After three weeks you can open the cage door and watch developments from a distance. Some Cockatiels will risk a flight quite quickly; others will take longer but don't force anything. Let the bird leave the cage of its own free will. Eventually, the bird's inquisitiveness will win and you will be able to witness its first flight.

Dangers and precautions

A bird flying free in a room can be confronted with any number of dangers. The most common are the following:
• Flying into a window or glass partition. A Cockatiel cannot see windows or glass partitions, so these need to be covered by a

Pied grey

net or some other type of curtain to prevent collisions or, in the worst case, a bird breaking its neck. In the event that it is regularly allowed to fly around the same room however a bird will often learn to recognise a partition and avoid it.

- Escape. The risk of a bird escaping is very high if somebody should forget to close the doors and windows. The chances of a bird surviving in the wild are relatively small. The temperature difference, especially during the cold weather of the autumn and winter, will make the bird sick. If attempts to quickly recapture it are unsuccessful it will soon die.
- Other pets. Cockatiels are very tolerant and can be kept with other birds, such as Budgerigars and Canaries, without any problem at all. Small pets such as Hamsters, Guinea Pigs and Rabbits rarely produce problems. Dogs and cats are different. Although dogs in general are not a problem, some individuals possess a keen hunting instinct and will do anything they can to catch a Cockatiel. Never leave a Cockatiel alone with a dog. Cats have a far more strongly developed hunting instinct than dogs, so strong in fact that a bird isn't even safe in a cage. Make sure that a Cockatiel and a cat are never left together alone in a room!
- Toxic plants. Cockatiels are

highly inquisitive and won't be able to resist taking a bite out of any house plant they may come across while they are flying around in a room. A number of plants are poisonous for them. Examples are yew, narcissus and primula. Make sure that no toxic plants are about when the bird is free.

- Unprotected fires. It goes almost without saying that unprotected fires pose a life-threatening danger to a Cockatiel flying around in the same room. Unprotected fires, such as a fireplace and lit candles, should be avoided whenever a bird is allowed out. Don't forget ceramic or electric hotplates either!
- Electricity cables. Cockatiels like to nibble on anything and everything including electric cables and wiring. Keep the bird under close observation whenever it is out of its cage to ensure that it doesn't start nibbling at wiring.
- Gaps between walls and furniture. Many a free-flying bird has died because it became jammed in one gap or another. Before releasing your bird you should carefully inspect the room and make any adjustments necessary.
- Sharp objects. Splinters, nails, cactus needles and other sharp projections can give a free-flying Cockatiel an ugly wound. Before you release the bird, make sure that there are no sharp objects in the room.

White-faced grey

Feeding

If you are to be able to enjoy keeping birds, especially Cockatiels, you will need to keep them healthy. Nothing is worse than having sick birds in a birdcage or indoor aviary.

What do they need?

It is important for the keeper to have some understanding of a –bird's nutritional needs because it's the keeper after all who –chooses the food. An adequate diet is important not only for general health but also for growth, development and the Cockatiel's strength.

A bird needs a diet that includes all of the nutrients its body –requires in the correct amounts and ratio. A number of nutrients are essential. These are proteins, fats, carbohydrates, water, minerals and vitamins. Depending upon the function that they fulfil in the body, they are categorised as nutrients used as building material, nutrients that bring in energy and protective nutrients.

Nutrients used as building material are those that a bird needs to build, rebuild and repair body tissue and cells. Proteins, minerals and water are classified as building material. Nutrients that bring in energy are those that a bird needs, amongst other things, to maintain its body temperature and use its muscles, for flying for example. Fats, carbohydrates and proteins are classified as nutrients that bring in energy. Protective nutrients are those that ensure that the body's processes function properly. Vitamins and minerals are classified as protective nutrients.

Proteins

Proteins belong to nutrients used as building material. They are very large and are built from many small molecules called amino acids. Due to their size, proteins need to be broken down into the amino acids before the bird's body can absorb them. A bird's body can absorb amino acids directly. There are 29 different known sorts of amino acids from which an incalculable number of proteins can be built. It can be compared with the letters of the alphabet from which an infinite number of words can be built. Proteins are therefore built up in a bird after they have first been broken down. There are actually 10 amino acids that a bird, also a Cockatiel, is unable to make. These amino acids are called essential amino acids. A temporary shortage of one of these amino acids will prevent the body from producing protein. Any long-term shortage will result in the bird's death. These essential amino acids need to be present in the Cockatiel's food.

No matter how well they are put together, seed mixes do not supply enough essential amino acids. Research has shown that Cockatiel feed needs to contain about 20% protein. Pure seed mixes contain only about 15% protein, which is clearly insufficient, so extra protein needs to be added.

Animal sources are richer in essential amino acids than vegetable sources so it is important that Cockatiels are given animal protein. Research shows that Cockatiels regularly eat insects in their natural environment in Australia. To ensure that Cockatiels receive enough protein, you should give them a daily concentrate containing essential amino acids in the correct proportions.

Minerals

Second on the list of building materials are minerals. Minimal amounts of minerals are present in a bird's body as trace elements. Minerals are involved in a number of the bird's essential processes and they form building blocks for various enzymes and hormones. As with amino acids, a number of minerals are essential for a bird's existence and here too a temporary or long-term shortfall will result in sickness and/or death.

Administering a dose of mineral trace elements needs to be done with precision bearing in mind that too much is just as bad as too little. Generally speaking, Cockatiels will receive enough minerals if you give them bird minerals, which can be obtained from pet shops. It is very important to serve bird minerals loose in a dish and refresh them once a week. Birds will only consume what they need and it will often appear that there are still sufficient minerals in the dish when in fact there are not. Cockatiels, like

Germinated seeds
with egg feed

other birds, are very selective and it may well be that the minerals they need at a particular moment have already been removed from the dish. It cannot be emphasised enough that a fresh supply of minerals must be given to them regularly, at least once a week. I personally sprinkle bird minerals over the feed in the feeding bowl twice a week to ensure that the birds receive the amount they need.

Apart from providing them with bird minerals, it is also important to provide them with natural products containing minerals. Examples are: kale, endive, milk powder (these can be mixed with energy food for example), egg yolk, wheat, cuttlebone and grit. Most prepared energy feeds have minerals added to them but this will generally be confirmed on the packaging.

Water

Third on the list of building materials is water. Water is exceptionally important for birds. Blood and muscle contain 95% and 70 to 80% water respectively. Each time nutrients are carried to or from a body cell, they are transported by water.

Water is present in nearly all foodstuffs. When energy is produced from food, water, for one thing, is produced as a bi-product. The water released however is not sufficient to answer a bird's entire needs so birds need to be given drinking water. The drinking water you supply should not be too cold. The drinking bowls should be cleaned at least once per week and the water should be replaced daily. Contaminated water is one of the most common causes of bird intestinal infection.

Fats

As already mentioned, a bird's body needs nutrients that bring energy in addition to nutrients that are used as building materials. Fats play an important role in this respect. Nutrients that bring energy are needed among other things to maintain a body temperature of 107.6 °F (42 °C) and for muscle power.

Fats are categorised as saturated and unsaturated fatty acids. The saturated fatty acids are in turn divided into fatty acids with long

carbon chains and fatty acids with short carbon chains. The unsaturated fatty acids are divided into monounsaturated fatty acids and polyunsaturated fatty acids.

As with amino acids and minerals, a number of fats are essential. Polyunsaturated fatty acids are essential for birds. The three most important polyunsaturated fatty acids are: linolic acid, linoleen acid and arachidonic acid.

Foods containing too much fat can make a Cockatiel ill. Fat slows down the production of digestive juices causing food to remain longer in the stomach. This causes the bird to feel full, stop eating and eventually suffer from a shortage of essential nutrients. Do not give a Cockatiel any more fat than is absolutely necessary.

Carbohydrates

In addition to fats, carbohydrates are a key source of energy. Carbohydrates contained in Cockatiel food are mainly vegetable carbohydrates. The most important carbohydrates that need to be present in the feed are divided into three groups: monosaccharides, disaccharides and polysaccharides.

Monosaccharides, such as glucose and fructose, are single sugars, which can be directly absorbed by a bird's body. This is not so for double sugars such as disaccharides

Cuttlebone

Feed dispenser

and polysaccharides. Double sugars have to be broken down by enzymes to single sugars before a bird's body can absorb them.

Cockatiels need to be given an adequate amount of carbohydrates in their food. Seeds, fruit and greens contain carbohydrates in sufficient quantities and these should be given daily. In addition to being considered as nutrients used as building material, proteins also contribute to a bird's energy requirements. This is why proteins are also classified as nutrients that bring in energy.

Vitamins

Following the groups of nutrients used as building material and nutrients that bring energy, comes the group of protective nutrients. In addition to minerals, vitamins are also classified as protective nutrients, and they play a key role in keeping birds healthy.

Water reservoir

Natural foodstuffs usually contain vitamins. Each vitamin has a specific task in a bird's body processes. Both a shortage and an excess of vitamins in bird food can be damaging and can cause abnormalities. As long as a bird receives a varied diet, it shouldn't suffer from a shortage of vitamins. When you are giving vitamins, as is the case with minerals, it's important that a good balance is achieved. The following products, amongst others, are rich

in one or more vitamins: Milk, milk powder, brown bread soaked in milk, egg yolk, germinated seeds, grain, seeds, soya flour, vegetables and fruits.

It will now be apparent that care is required if you prepare food for your Cockatiels yourself. Birdseeds are not all equally rich in proteins, fats, carbohydrates, minerals and vitamins. Feed containing the right balance of the ingredients mentioned can be made by mixing different varieties of seeds, but no seed mix is able of supplying the Cockatiel's complete need for amino acids, minerals, vitamins and essential fatty acids. Cockatiels kept in captivity need to be given extra amino acids, minerals, vitamins and essential fatty acids. As far as fatty acids are concerned, these could be given in the form of fresh vegetables. The need for essential amino acids can be satisfied by giving egg food (=strength food) and brown bread soaked in milk. Minerals can be given in the form of grit and cuttlebone or as bird minerals obtainable from shops. Minerals are added to the majority of egg foods. Minerals in the form of grit and/or bird minerals should be replaced at least once a week even if it appears that there is still enough in the dish. Vitamins are provided via the egg food. In practice, the majority of strength foods contain most of the essential vitamins making extra vitamins unnecessary. Because a seed mix is unable to meet the requirement for amino acids, minerals, vitamins and fatty acids, it is necessary to provide birds, amongst other things, with strength food/egg food to which these ingredients have been added.

Which food can I best give in practice?

When the food requirements are translated into a practical diet the Cockatiel's basic food consists of a large parrot seed mix and a quality egg feed/strength feed. A variety of pieces of fruit and greens should also be given on a daily basis. In addition to the food mentioned above, your birds should always have access to fresh cool drinking water, bird minerals (grit) and stomach gravel. If you want to give your Cockatiel something extra once in a while you can spoil it with some millet spray. Millet spray is easily digestible and all Cockatiels love it.

What is pellet food?

American ornithologists, biologists and bird breeders have cooperated over the years to develop pellet food for specific breeds of birds. Pellets are granules that contain all the nutrition that birds need. Commercial bird food manufacturers only make pellets for parrots and large parakeets simply because these birds have always been more popular and financially attractive than other sorts of cage and aviary birds. Feeding birds with pellets is in its infancy in our country and for many bird fanciers still a relatively unknown subject. Nevertheless, new and improved products come onto the market each year and it may be assumed that more and more bird fanciers will change to feeding their birds with pellets in the near future. The big advantage that comes from feeding with pellets is that once birds have changed over to a pellet diet the keeper can be sure that the birds are receiving all the nutrients necessary to keep them in good health.

Normal on nest

Cockatiels i
other colour

**As the years have passed spontaneous changes (mutations) have also produced Cockatiels in other colours.
Among hobby bird fanciers, all these colours have been given their own name.**

The most common Cockatiel colours are pastel, white-faced, pied, the black-eyed white and /or yellow, albino, lutino, cinnamon and pearl.

Pastel
The pastel Cockatiel is a bird with predominantly light grey, silvery coloured feathers.

White-faced
The red and yellow have disappeared from the white-faced Cockatiel's feathers. This has resulted in a white face especially so in cock birds. The cheeks of the hen are comple-tely grey. Because the yellow colour is missing, grey is a more pronounced colour in these birds.

Pied
Pied colour occurs in many animals

(and plants), including Cockatiels. The intensity of pied markings can be very variable. Cocks and hens are difficult to distinguish from one another because the pied markings make it difficult to see the diagonally striped tail of the hen. Sexing is often possible by carefully observing the birds' behaviour. Apart from their melodic courtship song, cocks exhibit clear macho behaviour that the hens do not.

Black-eyed white and/or yellow
This colour mutation has resulted from continuously crossing (pairing) pied Cockatiels with very little pigment with each other. This selective method of breeding finally produced a completely white and/or yellow

bird with black eyes. Cocks and hens are indistinguishable from one another. Sexing such birds is only possible by observing their behaviour, paying particular attention to the courtship song and macho behaviour of the cock. This macho behaviour consists of the cock walking perkily to and fro on the perch or the bottom of the cage or aviary with partially spread wings. Often the cock accompanies this behaviour with a melodic sounding courtship song.

Albino

The albino Cockatiel is an intense pure white bird with red eyes, as opposed to the black-eyed white described earlier, which, as the name suggests, has black eyes. The albino cocks and hens are indistinguishable from one another. Sexing is only possible by observing their behaviour. In addition to their melodic sounding courtship song, cocks exhibit a clear macho behaviour that the hens do not.

Lutino

The difference between the cock and the hen is clearly visible. The lutino hen's body colour is light yellow, whereas the cock is predominantly white with a yellow head. The orange-red ear patch and yellow cheek patch are more intensive in the cock than in the hen.

Cinnamon

The cinnamon Cockatiel is a bird

with a predominantly warm grey-brown colour. The differences between the cock and the hen are the same as the differences between the normal wild grey cock and the hen.

Pearl

The pearl Cockatiel has fine, regular markings on its back, wings, breast, flanks and around the vent. A strange phenomenon is that the cock's markings disappear when the bird is between seven and twelve months old, and all that remains is a grey bird. This is contrary to the hens that retain their pearl markings for life. Because of the above, sexing does not present any problems.

Lutino

Pied

Health and sickness

As long as Cockatiels are well cared for and provided with essential nutrition in sufficient quantities the chance of sickness and ailments is relatively small. Nevertheless, the chance is always there.

Infected eye

Recognising a sick bird

It is very important that the keeper notices as soon as possible when a bird is sick, so they need to be checked daily. Experience shows that even when birds don't appear to be in the best of health, too much time is lost before any corrective action is taken with the result that the birds do not receive the care they need at the moment they need it. Even though a 'suspect' bird may not be showing symptoms it must be captured and removed because it might well infect other birds, by way of its droppings for example. Timely recognition and corrective action is also important because sick birds eat little or nothing, and most birds are unable to last more than 24 hours without food.

If sickness is suspected it is important that the bird concerned be observed without the bird being aware of it.
This is because, if the bird should notice its keeper, it will behave differently, and often pull its feathers tightly against its body making it easy to conclude at such a moment that there is nothing wrong with it. While it appears that nothing is wrong, the moment the keeper is out of sight the bird will return to its sick-posture (closed eyes, fluffed feathers). Fluffed feathers are the most important sign that a bird is sick. A bird showing symptoms may already be in an advanced stage of sickness. In general terms, a bird that is visibly ill is also seriously ill.

Sick birds should be isolated in a hospital cage to prevent them from infecting others. The accommodation that the sick bird came from should be disinfected immediately. Feeding bowls, drinking fountains, perches and toys should receive special attention. The keeper should keep an eye out for a few days for signs of symptoms appearing in any other birds there may be.

Why do sick birds fluff their feathers?

A sick bird's temperature regulation is disrupted. As a result it will eat less than normal, lose weight and eventually find it difficult to maintain its body temperature at a normal level. The bird will attempt to retain heat by fluffing its feathers to insulate itself from the surrounding air. At this stage, it is important that the bird receives additional warmth. You can provide extra warmth by placing the bird in a hospital cage.

Sicknesses and disorders

A vet is naturally the best person to diagnose a sick bird, and the vet is more often than not also the person who will supply the medicine. Experience unfortunately shows that very few vets specialise in bird diseases. Another problem is that animals, unlike humans, can't tell you what is bothering them. Reaching a diagnosis, especially with birds, will not be easy. To help you on your way to recognising bird ailments, a description of a number of the most common ones, the associated symptoms and treatments, follows. Before you start doctoring for yourself however, make sure that the diagnosis you make is the correct one. If you are in any doubt at all you should always consult a vet. The same applies to ailments not mentioned in this book.

Anaemia

Anaemia can be the result of poor feeding or from the dreaded blood mite (red blood mite). The colour of the mucous membrane, skin and feet of a bird suffering from

anaemia is lighter than normal and it is often accompanied by weight loss.

Treatment: Improve the food. If there are signs of blood mite, the mites need to be eradicated with a mite spray. The mite spray must not be of a type that is harmful to birds (check the label for information). See also blood mite.

Blood mite (red bird mite)

The red bird mite is a very small, barely visible spider-like animal. They reproduce rapidly in warm weather, such as in the summer. Blood mites can appear in any birdhouse. Red bird mites hide in splits, cracks and holes during the day and emerge at night to suck the birds' blood. Once they have sucked themselves full, mites are recognisable as red dots. The presence of blood mites can be confirmed by wiping a knife blade along cracks and joins in the birdcage. If blood mites are present traces of blood will be visible on the blade of the knife. Mites do not present an immediate danger for birds, but they will weaken them over time.

Treatment: Blood mites should be eradicated with a mite spray. The mite spray must not be of a type that is harmful to birds (check the label for information). Blood mite sprays can be bought at pet shops.

Intestinal infection (enteritis)

Diarrhoea is one of the specific characteristics of intestinal infection.

In addition, birds with an intestinal infection will sit apathetically crumpled up with the head between the feathers, seriously sick. There can be any number of causes of intestinal infection.

The causes can be:

• *Spoiled food*

Food can become rancid if it is not stored properly. Damp egg food/energy food mix is liable to deterioration and decay, especially in hot weather. Birdseed must always be stored in a dry and cool condition. Give egg food and strength food as much as possible in a dry state. In warm weather, egg food mix should be replaced twice a day.

• *Too much iron in the food*

Greyish diarrhoea can be caused by water containing a high percentage of iron caused by water from rusty drinking bowls or well water for example. The solution is to use other drinking bowls or provide tap water.

• *Excessive fluid retention*

Causes for this can be: food that is too salty and/or providing too much green food. Check the ingredients of the food and temporarily stop providing green food.

• *Draughty accommodation*

Draught in the cage can cause birds to catch cold. Catching a cold nearly always goes hand in hand with an intestinal infection and therefore with diarrhoea. The simplest solution is draught-free accommodation.

Bird show

a hospital cage where the temperature should be about 95 °F (35 °C). Provide simple sugars so that the bird will regain energy. By providing simple sugars (dextrose for example), the bird will quickly recover and be able to eat normal food again. Simple sugars can best be diluted in water before being given. Any water given should not be too cold and it should be replaced twice a day. If the bird is too weak to drink, the sugar solution can be fed directly into the bird's crop with a crop needle. As food, you can provide antidiarrheal seeds. In addition you can give rusk crumbs mixed with a little charcoal powder or finely ground Norit tablets. The latter can also be mixed with antidiarrheal seeds. As soon as there is an improvement, you can stop giving the simple sugar dissolved in water. The temperature of the hospital cage should then be gradually reduced. It is always sensible to consult a vet. He or she will in all probability prescribe an antibiotic.

Diarrhoea
See intestinal infection (enteritis).

Overgrown beak
The lower beak sometimes continues growing, especially the beaks of hooked nosed birds, like Cockatiels. If nothing is done about it, the bird will soon encounter difficulty in peeling seeds and eventually starve to death.

• *Worms*
Whenever worms are present in a bird's intestines they excrete waste products. The excreta of these worms are toxic and can cause a bird to suffer from diarrhoea. The remedy is to administer a worming cure, closely following the instructions.

• *Poisoning*
Green food treated with insecticide can cause diarrhoea. Green food must always be washed thoroughly before it is given to birds.

Treatment for diarrhoea:
The first step is to wash any feathers covered in droppings with a sponge and lukewarm water. The sick bird should then be placed in

A bird that has caught a cold sits like a sad little ball crumpled up with its head between its feathers. Its wings hang and breathing is heavy. A slimy fluid often runs from the nose with the result that the bird often has to sneeze. *Therapy:* A bird with a cold should be placed in a hospital cage in which the temperature should be about 95 °F (35 °C). To provide an instant source of energy, give a single sugar such as dextrose. Single sugars will help the bird recover and return to eating a normal diet. Single sugars can best be given dissolved in water. The water must not be too cold and should be replaced twice a day. If the bird is too weak to drink by itself the solution can be given via the crop with a crop needle. Food should be given in the form of fruit, greens and a good seed mix. As soon as an improvement is visible, you can discontinue giving it the single sugars and water solution and start reducing the temperature in the hospital cage to room temperature. In serious cases it is advisable to consult a vet who will most likely prescribe an antibiotic.

Treatment: The beak can simply be cut with a pair of scissors or a pair of wire cutters.

Catching a cold

Catching a cold can be easily caused by large changes in temperature. Draughty and damp accommodation can also result in a cold. Another cause can be that the bird caught a cold after a bath.

Crop disease

Birds with crop disease constantly empty the content of the crop. The vomit consists of a sticky slime. By shaking its head to and fro the bird eventually covers its face, head and neck feathers with slimy vomit. Strangely enough, the feathers of a bird suffering from this disease remain smooth and tight against the body and don't become fluffed. A bird suffering from crop disease will die within 24 hours if treatment is not given.

Treatment: The only effective treatment for this disease is to administer an antibiotic, Vibravet for example. Antibiotics can be obtained from a vet.

Egg-binding

The term egg-binding applies if a female is unable to lay her eggs. A hen suffering from egg-binding will sit on the floor of the cage with fluffy feathers. Egg-binding often occurs with hens that are very young. Egg-binding can also be caused by large temperature changes and severe cold.

Treatment: A young hen suffering from egg-binding should be carefully captured. Once captured it should be wrapped in a damp, warm cloth and held over a pan of cooking water (watch out for scalds!). It is also advisable to lubricate the hen's vent with salad oil. Another treatment that can be used is to dip the hen's lower body alternately in lukewarm and cold water. It is advisable here too to lubricate the hen's vent with salad oil. A third possibility is to drip a few drops of salad oil into the hen's vent with a syringe from which the needle has been removed.

Remember that under no circumstances must you allow an egg to break inside the bird's body or the hen will die.

Eye infections

Eye infections may occasionally appear during the winter or in poorly ventilated rooms. In the case of the latter, the ventilation needs to be improved. Eye inflammations also occur in birds with overgrown nails. They can easily injure an eye, for example

when they are scratching their head. Check your bird's nails regularly to prevent eyes being injured by nails that are too long.

Treatment: Treat the affected eye with boracic lotion or boiled (tepid) water. Rinsing should be done with a water-soaked cotton wool wad. Each cotton wool pad should only be used once. A stubborn eye infection will need to be treated with antibiotic ointment or eye drops, Globenicol eye ointment or Neomycine eye drops for example, both of which can be obtained from a vet. Long nails need to be cut with scissors. Hold the nail up to the light so that you can see the blood vessels.

Ornithosis

Ornithosis is closely related to psittacosis, also known as parrot fever. Both illnesses are caused by a virus, but neither of them have disease-specific symptoms. The symptoms are very similar to those of flu. These are: fluffy feathers, breathlessness, infected eyes and a runny nose. The bird's feathers are often contaminated with the discharge from the nose. This sickness is infectious for both birds and humans!

Treatment: In the event of ornithosis or psittacosis consult a vet, who will prescribe antibiotics.

Leg fractures

Leg fractures can be caused by

Just born

accidents or fighting. Birds can also fracture a leg if startled, at night for example. A small night-light will reduce this risk.

Treatment: A broken leg needs to be immobilised. The leg can be immobilised using a straw that has been cut open lengthways or a feather shaft. The leg needs to be held straight and bandaged with one or two strips of Elastoplast. The bird should be housed separately in a cage without perches. The bird should be fitted with a neck collar to prevent it from pecking at the bandages. The bandages can be removed (carefully cut them off) after fourteen days.

Psittacosis
See Ornithosis.

**Knemidokoptic Mange
(scaly leg and face disease)**
Knemidokoptic mange, also called "cere mites", or "scaly leg and face disease" is caused by a microscopic mite called *Knemidokoptes pilae*. These mites live on the birds day and night, and cause large numbers of wart-like growths by tunnelling into the skin and feeding on the tissue. The symptoms are often first only seen in the beak's wax skin. The disease can be transmitted to other birds.

Treatment: An infected bird should be treated with an insecticide. Serious growths need to be treated for a few days by first soaking

them in insecticide. The wart-like growths can be covered with non-acidic Vaseline to deprive the mites of oxygen. Remember to keep the nostrils clear. Infected birds should be referred to a vet.

Feather lice and feather mites
Feather lice and feather mites can inhibit the development of growing feathers and cause feathers to fall out.

Treatment: To be able to make the right diagnosis, it is advisable to send or take feathers to the vet. The feathers should be placed in a tightly sealed plastic bag immediately after they have been plucked. Do not use any feathers that are lying on the floor of the cage because they may no longer carry any lice or mites! Feather lice and feather mites should be treated with an insecticide. In the event of feather lice or feather mites infection always consult a vet.

Injuries
Minor and major injuries can come about from fights and accidents quite easily. Small wounds heal spontaneously in most cases. Larger wounds, especially head wounds, need to be treated.

Treatment: Injured birds, just like all other sick birds, should be segregated to prevent other birds from pecking the wounds. Disinfect the wound(s) with tincture of iodine or another

disinfectant. The wound should be dressed if necessary and indeed if possible. The bird should be fitted with a neck collar to ensure that it doesn't peck at either the dressing or the wound. Large wounds will need to be stitched by a vet, which is why large wounds should always be referred to a vet.

Wing fractures
Wing fractures are almost always the result of accidents.

Treatment: If a bird sustains a wing fracture, the wing should be fixed to the body with a bandage. Three rolls will be necessary. The first roll is wrapped around the breast and wing roots. The second roll around the belly and the middle of the wings and the third roll around the tail and the wing tips. The bandages may be removed after about two weeks.

Worms
A worm infection occurs when a bird comes into contact with the worm eggs or larvae from infected birds. In the case of a chronic infection, a general deterioration

in condition and weight loss will be visible. If nothing is done to intervene, the bird will eventually die. Young birds are especially prone to worm infections. Worm infections often occur in the warm months of summer. A differentiation is made between worm infections of the intestines and worm infections of the airways.

Treatment: Birds infected with worms need to be treated with a wormer such as Ivermectine. The wormer must be administered strictly according to the instructions. A good way to worm a bird is to administer the remedy with the aid of a dropper or crop tube. Because of the danger of infection, the birdcage and/or aviary must be thoroughly cleaned while the worming is being carried out and new perches must be fitted. The drink and feeding bowls also need to be cleaned and disinfected. A worm treatment is mostly carried out in two phases.

Bird euthanasia

Helping with bird euthanasia is one of the most unpleasant things that a bird fancier can experience. Luckily most forms of illness and ailments are preventable but in those cases where a bird won't recover, the keeper will have to make a decision. In making the decision the question that needs to be asked is how much longer does the bird have to suffer in pain, and would it not be better to release it

from its suffering?
Helping an incurable or terminally sick bird to die quickly, and above all painlessly, can best be done using ether. Place the sick bird in a plastic bag and pour in a small amount of ether (about 0.5 fl oz or 15 ml is sufficient). Tie the bag closed. When the bird has died dispose of the body.

Disinfectants and pesticides

Disinfectants and pesticides are needed to combat sickness and vermin respectively. Both have a specific function. A disinfectant is used to cleanse a birdcage of bacteria, viruses and mould. A pesticide is used to combat both external parasites, such as lice and mites, and internal parasites, such as worms.

Disinfectants

It will be necessary to disinfect the complete birdcage, including the drinking and feeding bowls, whenever a bird catches an infectious disease. The sick bird must be captured and isolated without delay to be able to treat it more effectively and to prevent other birds from becoming infected. It is highly likely that the sick bird will have infected not only the birdcage but also the contents, which is why it is essential to thoroughly disinfect everything. Disinfectants need to be chosen with care. Follow the instructions on the packet closely.

Pesticides

As already mentioned, pesticides are used to combat vermin. Feather lice and blood mites are examples. Pesticides need to be chosen with care and the instructions printed on the label must be followed carefully.

What are the requirements of a hospital cage?

A hospital cage for Cockatiels should be about 50 cm high, 50 cm deep and 60 cm wide (20 x 20 x 24 inches). A good hospital cage is fitted with built-in heating, often in the form of an infrared lamp, and a thermometer is fitted on the inside. The warmth of an infrared lamp penetrates a few millimetres into the skin of a sick bird. Make sure that the hospital cage is easy to clean and disinfect.

It is also possible to put a sick bird into a regular cage and place the cage in a warm spot, for example on a central heating radiator or next to a stove. A thermometer is necessary to check the temperature.

Pied

White faced pearl

ball then the temperature is possibly still too low, if the bird starts panting with its beak open then temperature is too high.

Despite its need for warmth, the bird also needs to be able to move to a cooler spot. You also need to prevent too much light from entering the hospital cage, because too much light can irritate the bird. No matter where you place the cage, the location needs to be quiet and free of draughts and smoke.

Making your own hospital cage

The following points are important when you are constructing a hospital cage for Cockatiels:
- Use a cage (box) of about 24 x 20 x 20 inches (L x W x H) (60 x 50 x 50 cm). Make sure that the front of the cage can be fitted either with Perspex or bars. Fit the cage with a large door;
- Make the cage from material which is easy to clean (Trespa or aluminium for example);
- Fit the cage with a thermometer;
- Fit the cage with a heating source (an infrared lamp for example). It is also possible to place the cage above a central heating radiator or next to a stove. If you use an infrared lamp it is important that the bird has enough space in the cage to be able to escape from the heat source should it be in danger of

The temperature in a hospital cage needs to be about 95 °F (35 °C). The bird will generally drink more water due to the heat, so you will need to take this into account. The correct air temperature for a sick bird can be judged from its behaviour. If the bird remains huddled up like a

becoming too hot. The risk of overheating will be less of a problem if you use an open cage and place it either on or in front of a radiator;

• Fit a sliding tray under the bottom of the cage so that droppings can be easily removed;

• Make a gauze mesh screen to cover the sliding tray to prevent the bird from walking in its own droppings! The size of the perforations in the mesh should be suitable for the size of bird. The easiest way to fit the gauze is to bend it for support on two sides and lay it in the tray;

• Place a perch(es) so that the animal can access food and water easily. In the case of seriously ill birds it is a good idea to place a perch just above the wire mesh floor so that the bird's tail will rest on the mesh floor to help it maintain its balance. The thickness of a perch should be such that the bird is not quite able to close its claws completely around it;

• Lay waterproof material, plastic or greaseproof paper for example, in the bottom of the sliding tray so that droppings are easily seen.

About Pets

- The Border Collie
- The Boxer
- The Bulldog
- The Cavalier King Charles Spaniel
- The Cocker Spaniel
- The Dalmatian
- The Dobermann
- The English Springer Spaniel
- The German Shepherd
- The Golden Retriever
- The Jack Russell Terrier
- The Labrador Retriever
- The Puppy
- The Rottweiler
- The Siberian Husky
- The Shih Tzu
- The Stafforshire Bull Terrier
- The Yorkshire Terrier
- The African Grey Parrot
- The Canary
- The Budgerigar
- The Cockatiel
- The Finches
- The Lovebird
- The Parrot
- The Kitten
- The Cat
- The Siamese cats
- The Persian cat
- The Chipmunk
- The Dwarf Hamster
- The Dwarf Rabbit
- The Ferret
- The Gerbil
- The Guinea Pig
- The Hamster
- The Mouse
- The Rabbit
- The Rat
- The Goldfish
- The Tropical Fish
- The Snake
- The Tortoise

Key features of the series are:
- Most affordable books
- Packed with hands-on information
- Well written by experts
- Easy to understand language
- Full colour original photography
- 70 to 110 photos
- All one needs to know to care well for one's pet
- Trusted authors, veterinary consultants, breed and species expert authorities
- Appropriate for first time pet owners
- Interesting detailed information for pet professionals
- Title range includes books for advanced pet owners and breeders
- Includes useful addresses, veterinary data, breed standards.

about pets

The Cockatiel

Scientific name:	*Nymphicus hollandicus*
Sub-species:	None
Origin:	Australia
Area of distribution:	All of Australia with the exception of coastal areas in the North, East, South and parts of the West
Habitat:	Open wooded savannahs, edges of woods close to flowing water, grassy desert-like land, city parks
Size:	12 to 13 inches (32 to 34 cm)
Distinguishing sexual characteristics:	The hen has a lighter coloured head and in general is much less striking than the cock. The underside of the hen's tail is striped irregularly yellow. The underside of the cock's tail is pure black.
Character:	Placid and even-tempered
Behaviour vs. other aviary birds:	Peaceable
Feeding in the wild:	Seeds from grasses and weeds, blossom nectar, berries, nuts, leaf buds, insects and larvae
Feeding in captivity:	Seed mix for large parakeets, egg food, greens and fruit (2 to 3 x per week), bird minerals, sharp stomach gravel
Minimum cage dimensions:	L 40 x W 24 x H 32 inches (100 x 60 x 80 cm)
Sexual maturity:	After one year
Length of sexual maturity:	About 15 years but longer is not uncommon
Most common colours:	Pastel, white-cheek, pied, 'black-eyed', lutino, cinnamon and pearl